The Human Contract

The Human Contract

Poems by

Sarah Dickenson Snyder

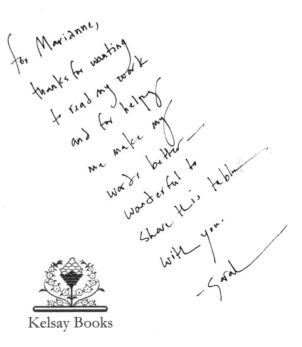

For Marianne,
thanks for wanting
to read my work
and for helping
me make my
words better—
wonderful to
share this table
with you.

—Sarah

Kelsay Books

Cover photograph: Sara Dickenson Snyder

ISBN: 13-978-1-945752-32-2

Kelsay Books
Aldrich Press
www.kelsaybooks.com

For my mother and father

And for Ben and Abby and David
(who have made me better)

Acknowledgments

Thank you to the magazines and anthologies that first printed the following poems that appear in this collection:

The Comstock Review: "Splinter," "Half-Life Hibernation," and "Blessing For My Daughter Leaving for School" (previously "When She Leaves")
Broken Bridge Review: "Class Picture Day"
Mothering Magazine: "Their Hair"
Zeugma Magazine: "My Mother" part iii
Bloodroot Literary Magazine: "The Dead Pour Out of Rain" and "Starting to Carve My Mother's Grave Stone"
The Senior Times: "Blessing"
West Trade Review: "In the Newspaper This Morning"
Mothers Always Write: "To My Mother" (previously "Fierce"), "Lord & Taylor," "What's Lost," and "Close Reading"
The Main Street Rag: "Birthday Photograph"
Snapdragon Magazine: "Ever After"
Litbreak Magazine: "What I Would Do Were I in an Avalanche" (previously "Avalanche"), "My Father" part ii, "The Human Contract" (previously "Angelology"), "Fortune Telling," and "Winning"
Necessity is a Mother: Toolbox Tales When All Else Fails: "I'm Taking Fish Sticks out of the Freezer"
Damfino Press: "What Else Happened the Year I Negotiated with Darkness and Entered Air" (previously "1954")
Oddball Magazine: "White Towel Blurred With Blood" (previously "The Human Contract")
WomensArts Quarterly Journal: "Rodeo"

Awards from The Poetry Society of Vermont:

"For My Mother" received the Marian Gleason Memorial Award 2015
"Junior High" received the Goldstein Memorial Award 2015
"Dead Fawn Curled in a Pool under Old City Falls" received the J. Richard Berry Memorial Award 2016
"Summer Fog" received the Goldstein Memorial Award 2016

With many thanks to those who have read my work and pushed it into better places: Barbara Helfgott Hyett, Arthur Sze, Wendy Drexler, Shana Hill, Julia Tait Dickenson, Anne Douglass, Jen Hamilton, Jess Brennan, Laura Foley, Hal Coughlin, Lys Weiss, and many others around a table at Poem Works, the Tuckerbox, and the Bread Loaf Writers' Conference.

Contents

Part III

Part I

In the Parking Lot after School

I need to right
myself. So much has happened
in an avalanche—bank over-
drafts, students yelling, *Fuck you!*

Oh, and an abortion, a whine deep
within me. I sit in my car,
lean into the steering wheel,
too much to tell—

a car of pain. I'm cold,
I should turn on
the engine, let the vents
warm, but I'm frozen.

On the seat beside me,
my canvas bag bloats with books,
pens, the five folders of papers
I will correct tonight,

propped up by pillows,
still cold, pen marks
staining sheets
I'll wash someday.

The Human Contract

Alone, my car window rolled down,
a pack of gum to chew, keeping me awake,
the radio loud and grainy on a late night
warmed inside from a weekend with my boyfriend,
everything as it should be on this dark corridor
of highway, another forty-five minutes
to Cundy's Harbor and sleep. But nothing
is as it should be for long.

A sudden cough, a deep inhale, and I sucked
back the hunk of gum, a cork, suffocating me
at seventy miles an hour. My mind hurled
to my obituary scrolled
in script on newsprint:

Sarah Stelle Dickenson died
from choking on several pieces
of Trident Sugarless Gum
between Wells and Kennebunk.

I'm going to die—I press my foot hard
on the accelerator, see red taillights,
drive alongside that van, jam my hand
on the horn, both of us drive—slide
to the shoulder, an angel jumped out,
pulled me to him, my back against his chest—
a sudden thrust of fists below my ribs unhinged
the wad. We stood there on the side
of the highway like that, me shaking,
him, holding me backward.

Odysseus and Women

—after Homer

i.
With Kalypso he is merely a man
in her *sea-hollowed caves*, and she—
a weaver of ruin. *She craved him*
for her own and *clung,* casting spells
in darkness. He can rationalize—
she's a goddess, and so he becomes deified,
heroic. But he's just a man on a tropical island
with a sea nymph and no ship to mount the sea.

ii.
With Athena he wants to rise
toward heaven—god-like, waits like a cloud
for her to finish pretending to be mortal. He imagines
the sand, his wife's clean voice, his son's hand
so small in his, being weightless but moored.

iii.
With Penelope he is an old man. When he speaks,
the skin of her pale face grows moist.
And her trick to know him—the immovable trunk,
an olive tree he'd *hewed and shaped* into a bedpost.
The bed he must have dreamed
of after so many years on an endless sea,
nothing forgotten—so pulled to her.
And she to him. *There are secret signs we know,*
we two, she says. So much can be forgiven.

My Mother's Wedding Dress

I remember nothing
of what we had for lunch

that day, nor the view
of the Golden Gate Bridge

I'd come to love, just my waiting
for the right time to ask if I could wear

the silken dress I'd seen encased in plastic
at the back of her closet my whole life—

had imagined this moment for weeks.
No! You can't wear my wedding dress.

You're getting married in August.
That dress was for November,

she said as she brushed off
bread crumbs, nothing left

on the table but the clean
white cloth beneath.

South Strafford, August 15, 1987

A Vermont morning,
so blue as if

a furnace were churning
out a new color with clouds

outlined in mythology—
a woman and a man

about to thread themselves
together—had there been

worn earth that led
to this juncture

or rungs of a ladder
climbed unaware

to stand on
the just-mown edge,

hammering hand-painted signs
along the side of the road.

Honey Moon

Those photographs of us, entwined,
Maui horizon behind. We ate wedges

of pineapple and thick slices of banana bread
with a backdrop of fringed palms, a crisp moon,

and a simmering volcano. I have the recipe
and make The Coconut Inn bread still,

stirring a beginning, adding
shredded coconut, almond extract—

allowing butter to soften, bananas to ripen,
no need to measure the flour or honey.

When My Husband is Away for a Week

I walk in the silent house laden with bags
some groceries—bananas, one just-ripe tomato,

feta cheese, thick bread. The porcelain bowl
on the counter is nearly full—

apples, some peaches, two lemons.
I add the tomato, pull out bananas from the bag,

slip them on top. Like
two smooth legs, they part.

First Bath

It's a small
basin
in the kitchen sink

on Desmond Street—
I sluice warm
water all over

her, cup her head
in my palm,
touch each

tiny finger
nail. A cleansing
of all

I didn't—
leaving undiminished
holiness.

To My Mother

Today my daughter
climbs her way up your chair,

lifting her little legs,
pulling up with her arms

as you were working
the Sunday puzzle.

When she has found your lap
at last, *Hug me, Granny,*

she demands. Fierce words
I never dared try.

Close Reading

A son lost in this space,
mesmerized, content to sit
close to a bookshelf as if it offers heat

& presents to open. Each page turned
with small fingers, gliding eyes across
an opened expanse, lifting paper until

he begins another. Books pile by his side—
a tower he's building about to buckle,
the weight of what he's doing on his own.

Set Free

The three of us are cancelling
winter—no snow and cold today.
We pull down the shades, close the curtains.

Every lamp, every bulb filament flickers,
spraying light inside. We take out
big sheets of paper, markers, plastic tubs

of paint and brushes to make a carpet of art
on the kitchen floor: huge circles of sun
bursting with rays and palm trees and

ocean—so much blue and green.
Summer—we tape it over
the covered windows,

put on bathing suits, bring the beach
towels down from the closet to the living room,
slather on lotion, find the cooler in the basement,

fill it with ice, grapes, chips in plastic bags,
cheese sandwiches, and juice boxes.
We pick our favorite books, put on sunglasses,

turn up the music loud—
laughter rises
toward our suns—a miracle.

Waiting for My Prescription at CVS

At the magazine aisle, I pick
up a copy of *Vogue*, see women
glistening—all neck and legs,

sultry blades of grass
weaving envy in me.
Nothing exotic

about the spread
of my skin, breasts
emptied of milk.

Even a crying baby
can unleash a twinge
in me. How my breasts

once satiated, sustained.
But I can't stop flipping
the silky pages, note a lip color—

Kinda Sexy or Pretty in Plum,
search for that
in the make-up aisle.

Mortal Mothering

When my children leave
for school, I touch their small wrists,

sweep their hair with my hand.
Fingertips, tacit mantras:

stay on the sidewalk, let no one
tease you, you are wanted, loved.

Such feeble armor—
even less than a dusting

of soil over tulip bulbs
before the rough hold of winter.

In the Newspaper This Morning

She jumped
twenty-four stories,

holding her nine-month-old baby,
left two notes, one inside

the apartment and one taped
to the baby. That's what I can't let go of,

not the ledge or the leap
but imagining her searching

for two slips of paper,
the roll of tape, lifting dishes

on the kitchen counter
opening drawers

and sifting through
them to find the roll of tape,

then pressing the tape
on the cotton onesie

of the baby. She must have needed
two or three pieces of tape,

enough to wrap a present—
all before she leapt.

I'm Taking Fish Sticks out of the Freezer

How many do you want, Abby?
Five, her head down near the "V" of her book.
How about you, David?

Six, he says looking up from *Calvin and Hobbes*.
Did you say 'sex'? Abby asks, eyes wide.
No, he says quietly.

What do you know about 'sex'? I ask without a clear plan.
Allie told me about it last night at the sleep over.
What did she say? David asks and I think.

Sex is when two people are naked in bed, she says.
I slide the pan in the oven, close the door,
That's true, I say. Silence, then she asks,

Have you done sex, Mom?
Yes, I have, I say. More silence.
Why? she asks.

Why? I repeat. Stalling—I can't say
sex feels so perfect because I disappear.
Well, sex is how babies get made, I say instead.

They seem satisfied, but no, David is calculating
as usual, eager to be right,
You've done it twice!"

True-ish. *Yes, yes I have,*
I say. We're good, we can move on—
everyone feels fine.

Can two boys do sex? Or two girls? he asks.
Yes they can, but they won't
make babies, I say.

I'm hungry, Abby says.
Me, too, David says,
the timer about to ring.

Their Hair

It's evening,
the windows are dark
rectangles, the kitchen
washed in light.

Both of them
are doing homework
at the table as I cook.
I move by him,

bend to smell
the top of his head,
breathe in, know
his smell.

I touch
hers,
linger in
its shine.

One Summer in Ireland Nothing Went Wrong

The sun shone almost every day
on Dingle Bay, the dark sea cleared

to green. Dolphins followed our boat
to the Skelligs with only blue sky

over the beehived buildings
where monks spoke to God.

In the hills above the Black Spot Pub
in County Kerry, we drank water

from a holy spring. Each of us sipping
from the stout glass on the rock ledge.

On the beach—stones for the taking,
blue and purple, smooth and stacked

in our living room on an end table
for me to remember how a country

can make a good impression,
how we can remember a storm

or the rainbow right after, something
arcing over us, a temporary end to darkness.

My Daughter's First Day of Middle School

I wake to lines of light
and blinds and know

I will rise but stay, still warm
and hear her opening

heavy wooden drawers
that creak against their frames.

Now she's at the full-length
mirror in the hallway.

Pretending to sleep, I watch her
through my door. She bends

at the waist, tosses her cloud of light
brown hair, stands to look at herself,

pressing her lips to a pout—
a sultry stare she's seen in magazines,

I'm sure, She's gone, a blur. More zipping,
buttoning. She's back—black pants, black sweater,

a scarf of blue, new shoes.
Ten, twelve more versions of this show.

And one will work, a scattered parade
of possibility fallen in her wake.

Winning

Yet another thing I'll never win—*The New Yorker*
cartoon I create a caption for. And how many
times have I entered the bring-your-own-bag
raffle at Trader Joe's. And yesterday, I mailed
three poems in a manila envelope
to the Red Berry Editions Valentine's
Day Poetry Contest along with a self-
addressed, stamped envelope, a fifteen-dollar
check and what I hope is a pithy cover letter—
all riding in a mail truck, bound for
a cargo plane to California where they will be
walked to the desk of the Red Berry Editions
editor who will read my poems. I want her
to read them out loud—so loudly I will hear her.

Blessing for My Daughter Leaving for School

You will swim with sharks,
harvest sponges, try to save

lionfish, turtles, the endless sea.
You will breathe underwater,

Daughter who learned
to breathe underwater in me.

Everything tender
must be released.

What's Lost

I must be hard
on rings to lose
so many stones:

an amethyst untucked
from its circle of gold,
the first small pearl

in a row of five,
an oval of lapis set
in silver—all lost.

My children's baby teeth
placed under their pillows,
lost and kept—

the warm smell of their skin,
into the curve of my hip,
my neck, my life.

And tulip petals falling
from the vase in the slanted
light of dusk.

Part II

Rodeo

The metal gate is glinting, cowboys stirring
up dust. My mother has reached her seat
in the bleachers, and I fold her walker,

set it aside. The first rider is impatient.
His hands tighten on the leather horn
of his saddle—his shirt, just-ironed crisp.

My mother smiles at him.
The second rider lassoes a calf.
Chaps and boots and honest cowboy hat

blur as he ties the hooves. My mother
keeps her breathing measured. A third
cowboy arcs out and up, looks

desperate as the bronco tosses
him to his place on earth. My mother
leans into the sun—a blossom.

Half-Life Hibernation

My mother sits in a state of half-alive
at a table stacked with several Sudoku books,
cooking magazines, the Sunday *New York Times* folded

to the puzzle, three thick books to help her solve
this week's version, a phone on her left side,
worn nubs of pencils on her right, a vase of roses

in varying stages of rusted edged petals, a stout glass
of rum with four ice cubes. So little hair surrounds a face
puffed by Tarceva, ice cream, and disappointment. But those eyes—

they aren't hibernating. I have a hard time looking
directly into them because we both know too much,
know how deep she is in her cave.

My Father

i. Wakes, decides
   not to put in his hearing aids

   which are right there
   on the round table beside his bed.

   The little buds cost thousands
   and have batteries that he needs

   help finding
   at the pharmacy, batteries

   so small two are lost
   in the carpet at his feet.

   He can't bend over
   to get them.

   Today, he'd rather not hear
   my mother reminding him

   how far away he is
   from the man he was.

ii. When we walked away
    from him in his room

    to eat a spinach salad—
    walked out of his hearing,

    out of his smelling,
    his room silent of us,

    he could untether
    himself—nothing to hold him here.

My Mother

i. I steady her
   wheelchair behind her

   in the bathroom
   as she brushes her teeth,

   one hand on the counter,
   the other moving

   her moving toothbrush.
   She makes a sound,

   an *uhhing* sound, her labored
   breath as toothpaste foams

   and drips from her lip—
   not satisfaction exactly,

   but something almost sweet
   in her mouth.

ii. The hospital johnny rides up her splayed,
    bloated legs and slips off her shoulder
    where a lurid bruise maps

    the metal rod that holds her bones
    together. I lean over her as she sleeps,
    hold the edge of the thin cotton, pull it

    back to her, cover her chest,
    her thighs—whatever I can—
    without waking her.

iii. She lies tucked in, a neatened,
    statue, her white nightgown

    buttoned high. Her face lacquered
    in a sheen. Eyelids look too large,

    her nose well-defined,
    a clear tidemark.

    I whisper, kiss her
    forehead, skin like a leaf

    falling, slips and sways
    away in wind.

iv. To go on—buttoning
    the small buttons, folding death

    into a little square
    I can put away.

Dead Fawn Curled in a Pool under Old City Falls

Maybe she didn't know
where the river fell

and so she must have flown,
puff of her tail high and white.

Maybe we will sail
in the flutter of a leap

toward a fragile point—
leave our bodies

behind, encased
and chaste.

For My Mother

In the upstairs bathroom
I keep her wooden hairbrush

in the medicine cabinet—
an artifact in a little

mirrored museum.
No hair left among the bristles—

she had no hair
for years. I close my eyes,

breathe the brush the way
I inhale lilacs, almond cake.

Nothing of her
is left. Not a scent.

Starting to Carve My Mother's Grave Stone

I draw with a T-square, pencil
the letters in white before I begin—
the chisel in my left hand,
the wooden mallet in my right.

I run a v-cut, an unhindered gallop,
leaving only a slight residue
of stone dust, one line, a second—
clean lines that slant,

meet at the point
of a V—I force myself
to say aloud *Virginia*,
my mother's given name.

No one ever called her that—
too formal for someone
who wore sneakers,
drank Mount Gay rum,

and yelled at the Eagles
and Flyers on TV—
she was always *Jinny*,
always there.

At the Farmers Market

My sister thinks she sees our dead mother
in late summer at the farmer's market.

Julia sits behind her booth of bracelets
and necklaces—fresh water pearled, silver clasped.

One aisle over our mother moves past
the crowded stalls, pauses to feel

an heirloom tomato she lifts to gauge
its heft and color, digs into her

orange leather wallet, pulls out a bill
and change and pays. She sees some stacks

of brownies in the midst of loaves of bread
and buys one for the ride home.

Our mother, returned, filling
a canvas bag again.

The Dead Pour Out of Rain

They fill hollow
prophesies, endlessly
loosened as the language

of wind and trees.
A whoosh, unwavering.
As for time—

they let that be the end
of that. They move
into roots because they can

sink deeply—making
dirt and rock
unearth themselves.

They compress,
relinquish bits of bone
where we kneel and sift.

Watching You Through the Window

—for my husband

Woodpeckers have hollowed
out the trunk of the linden.

Its leafless branches
dangle and sway.

You go out with your rake,
gather rocks, small branches—

flotsam of storms. Use that rake
to uproot weeds in the driveway,

scrape mold and moss grown
over brick steps. Pull thick muck

from stuck gutters. Saplings
severed for more light,

and now a motor—you're on
the tractor, heading down

to the field, inscribing rows
and rows of where you've been.

Where They Rest

I swim with my dead parents,
burned to white ash and bits of bone—
poured into our pond as powder

until water turned them
to feathery clouds. I love the color
of the water—Rishikesh green,

so clean. I glide with them, tadpoles,
slippery sleeves of grass, or maybe they
have settled in the sediment below.

My Eggs

Four are worth mentioning.
Two were vacuumed out
at the same Planned Parenthood
two years apart.

Another became Abby.
And another became David.

The others slid into soft
lining, becoming blood—
years of those.

And then a hysterectomy—
fallopian tubes, womb & one ovary
all gone. Now just an ovary—
a small basket of no eggs.

Ever After

Rinsing rice, my hands
are my mother's—

rice swirling
through our fingers,

as I bathe the grains,
in the steel pot

and pour out clouded
water, fill the pot again,

again until the water clears.
I hold a sweating zucchini

and her ceramic knife,
lever its sharpness—

press her blade and make
what she has made.

MRI Waiting Room

I breathe through my nose,
as I have been taught in yoga.

I reach for the book I brought along,
then stand. *I think I will have that*

valium, actually, I say
to a woman behind the counter.

(Spelunking is a word I like a lot,
but I will never crawl through caves.

I endured Sebastian Faulk's *Birdsong*—
so full of tunnel warfare—for the writing.)

And the womb—my first
crucible—busting

out toward a small
aperture of light.

Wood Stove Cleaning

Many screws and sheaths of metal
on a tarp—and every scrap of dust
and soot removed. This stranger in my home

is taking so long—I read about the couple
on another mountain. Professors—the wife
making a tomato sauce, the husband reading in the den,

two young men knock on their door.
No one alive inside hours later.
My ribs yield and I say, *Coffee?*

I'm good, he says, packing up his stuff.
I did want a clean stove—a clean heart.
Through the window prayer flags flutter.

Summer Fog

At the top of Jericho Street
where the road becomes dirt,
fog conceals the world below—

no White River,
no hard curves of highway,
no houses beyond the Lyman farm.

When the fog burns off,
each shrouded life will
emerge undiminished.

But this moment I see
only the unveiled pool of a sky,
three deer grazing in the high

meadow, & smell sweet hay,
hear the sound of stone
on stone as I pass by.

Blessing

In Chiang Mai at a temple up steep steps
a monk dunks long, stiff reeds
into a wooden bowl and shakes
holy water over me.

In Limpopo Province Sister Eugenia
lifts her finger from the bowl of sacred oil
presses the tip on my forehead,
Safe passage, she says.

In bed we join the sky
with ribs and stars—
collapse into
the cure of night.

Fortune Telling

My palm looks smooth
in her hand. She turns

it over, the other side roped
with veins and wrinkles,

speckled with age. *Your life
line merges into the head*

line, she says. So much lives
in my mind—my father's half

smile, my mother's image
in a dressing room mirror

wide enough for her wheelchair—
I think I was beautiful once,

she said to me, to her.
And there—the marriage line,

just below my pinky, one slight
indentation—almost unseen

on the edge of my palm
an immutable crease,

not like the dimple my mom tried
to make in her cheek as a child—

slept on the side of a penny—
her mark didn't stay.

Part III

What Else Happened the Year I Negotiated with Darkness and Entered Air

Color TV launched, another new
cluster lit—propelled into perpetuity.

I arrived to Walter Cronkite's voice—
his first and mine to fill our home, to smell

the first TV dinner from Swanson
and Sons, and see Hank Aaron

of the Braves, the *Seventh Samurai*'s
symbols—dark roads to a secret story,

and in Sylacaugh, Alabama, a woman
named Ann Hodges was napping on her couch

(thankfully covered in quilts) when a softball-
sized meteorite broke through

the ceiling, bounced off her radio
and hit her in the hip, leaving

only a bruise, a mark from space.
And I, I was measured, unfettered.

The Babysitter Said They'd Be Home Soon

It's been a week without them here—
I'm waiting, warmed by the picture window sun
behind the love seat,

where Dad proposed to Mom
(when Mum-mum had the couch).
I feel a prickle—the sharp end

of a feather or a porcupine
quill through the fabric
of the seat I climb.

I see a plane in a patch
of sky, reach
a fingertip up high,

press it hard—
pull them home
across the glass.

After Their Party

It was sneak-down time
as my sister and I descended

the steps knowing where to place
a foot on each surface to diminish

the creak, creating a soft syncopation
down the fourteen stairs. It was Sunday,

birds heard but muffled through glass
and curtain. Though no cigarette smoke

lingered, the smell did in little mountains
of ashes and lipstick-stained butts in ashtrays

on each end table in the living room. We tasted
a couple, spit them out, lifted remaining sips of drinks,

coughed them out, too, and headed to the kitchen
for Frosted Flakes, milk, and almost muted cartoons.

Lord & Taylor

Anne and I wore red velvet dresses
and the Christmas corsages

my father brought home in boxes,
put in the refrigerator until my mother

pinned them on our winter wool coats.
Lord & Taylor was filled with "Winter Wonderland"

and the escalator, my favorite part.
I remember touching the shiny ridges

of the moving stairs near the top when the hem
of my dress slipped into the slight opening.

My father grabbed me at the waist, yanked me
out of danger. But the dress my mom had finished

that morning (making me stand too long,
her sitting on the floor with pins in her mouth,

saying, *Turn, just a little*
without moving her lips) was ruined.

Christmas

I remember a mini Whitman's
Sampler in my Christmas stocking,

along with a navel orange
down at the very bottom of the toe.

There was lot more stuff, but those two
were in every stocking I had as a child—

four chocolate treats (one of which
I'd throw away—the liquid cherry centered one).

Birthday Photograph

I am in front because I want
to be closer to my mother,
closer than she'll ever let me be.

Behind me—my friends Nancy, Kathy,
whose mother had died
of cancer, and Johnny, who gave me

the plastic palomino
I told him I wanted.
This line of friends

snakes back to my siblings—
everyone waiting to eat cake
on my birthday.

I am the only blurry one—
standing too near the camera
to be seen clearly.

Splinter

Sulfur in the air after my mother
strikes a match to sterilize, darken

the point of a needle. She focuses
on my foot cradled in her hand.

I'm sitting on a stool in that silly
looking Easter dress,

wide scalloped collar
scratchy and stiff.

Hold still, she says
before she hurts me.

My Sister Falls Asleep

But my mother keeps
reading *The Secret Garden*
on the edge of my bed.

I lie on my side, make myself
small next to her,
the thick book in her lap.

The lamp between
the twin beds is on—
her eyes, downcast.

I huddle near her voice, worry for Mary—
her parents dead, a cousin confined to a wheelchair,
and a garden to cure—a mansion of secrets.

Class Picture Day

In the photograph I am standing
up against the sitting Mrs. Zucaucus,
whose arm skin jiggled when she wrote on the board.

My hand is behind her, touching the soft pillows
of her back. I loved her flowered dress,
the belt's enormous job,

her silver curls knowing about gravity.
We're in the upper left corner—
no space between us.

White Towel Blurred With Blood

All morning I'd practiced—
      hair tucked in a cap,
my tank suit sagging—

six years old in the deep end.
      Toes gripping a curved edge
of rough cement, heels hovered

over water, palms pressed
      against my thighs, eyes closed,
leaping far from the lip

of the pool. Over and over,
      I jumped backwards, swam to the side
and pulled my body up the silver steps.

Perfected, I called to a circle of moms
      in sunglasses, *Look!*
I remember the doctor stitching my chin.

I remember stopping
      for a box of fudge
on the way home—

and from then on,
      always seeking the right
distance from the sun.

Etched Somewhere

Once Mrs. Armstrong chose me
to clean the erasers on the playground

just outside our classroom window.
I remember clapping the two together

like cymbals against the sky, sending
signals—puffs of dust—

I have been chosen! Mrs. Armstrong
who could stop Billy Martin's foot tapping

with a slight rise of an eyebrow picked me.
I walked back into the room, her perfume

like flowers in our world. She smiled as
I placed the cleaned erasers on the chalk tray

and looked out to the small sea of faces to see
an empty desk—my place.

Cigar

My grandfather lost most
of his money in the Crash,

just after he'd bought a seat
on the New York Stock Exchange,

was still in debt when he died
forty years later, my father told me.

His voice filled our house, our dining room,
the meal over as we waited for him

to unwrap a cigar, first that crinkle
of cellophane, then the paper ring he'd slide

off and slip into his hand as the four of us
waited. Who would he give it to—

who would get to wear the ring,
have its papery presence all night.

Almost Another

The four of us must have begged relentlessly
for a dog for a father with asthma to acquiesce.

A wire hair fox terrier arrived—Jams,
an acronym of our names.

But three weeks into training Jams to fetch,
sit, stay, three weeks of inhaling her dogness

after dinner on the couch, my dad took to bed
allergic to her saliva, too. I remember

the family pulling out of our driveway,
taking Jams away, along with her

flannel bed, her shiny bowl, her—
her wild beating heart next to me.

Groundwork

When I screamed, my father ran in,
cupped the half-dead black bird
in his hands. *I'll put it out of its misery*, he said.

I didn't go into the garage with him
and that dark mess of blood and one still-flapping wing
my cat had brought to me.

Did he slam a hatchet on the feathered curve of a neck?
Or hammer its head, maybe smash it with a shovel
on the cement floor? Or shove it in a garbage bag

still alive, knowing it would suffocate.
This is how I learned about mercy—
from a father who killed a bird to save it.

Junior High

It's the last dance of the night—a slow one,
of course. Jim Porter's rough lapel
against my cheek but I wish it were Paul Davis

whose tie is loosened but still knotted, standing
on the side. We rock from foot to foot
to "Young Girl" by Gary Puckett & the Union Gap

in this cavernous, darkened gym. I want someone
whose love for me is way out of line,
I lace fingers behind Jim's neck,

and his hands sweat the small of my back.
There are teachers posted at every exit
sign. I'm sure some girl is crying

in the bathroom circled by friends.
Not me. I'm swaying, waiting, maybe
for what never happened.

Family Room

On good nights we spilled into the family room
after dinner to watch TV, my brother taking

the best chair, my parents on the couch, Anne,
Julia, and I, lying on the shag rug, sprawled

over pillows. On *Laugh In* a grown man in a yellow
slicker rides a tricycle, his giant legs pumping fast,

as he grips the silver handle bars, zooming down
the sidewalk and splat!—both onto theirs sides,

one wheel in the air spinning like a small moon—
all of us laughing—a laughing room,

a laughing house. A laughing car—my father
at the wheel, whirling us around the grassy circle

on Golf View Road, no seat belts,
all four of us kids in the back, laughing,

my sister leaning her head out one window
of our station wagon, me flinging my head out

the other, our hair flapping like flags
until my mother yelled, *Stop!*

South Strafford

Come on in, Dad would say at the front door,
a screen door with a satisfying slap—

a summer slap, the slap of smells,
just-cut grass and rifts of leaves.

Through the threshold, our penciled
heights on the door molding never painted.

Come on in and have a drink, he'd say. And
evening would commence, a slab of beef

on the grill, zucchini and cheese bubbling
in the oven, the deep salad bowl

of loose greens and August
tomatoes, beer bottles perspiring

on the railing of the deck as the sun
fell behind Whitcomb's Hill.

Our family and several others tucked in
a small house or spilling out, someone

playing ring toss under the eaves where
the wasps buzzed but rarely stung.

I Used to Be

Sally with pigtails.
Sally in a round collared blouse.
Sally who had a birthmark,

a small puddle planted on her cheek.
Sally who wanted to be an only child
always sitting in the front seat

between her parents, not crammed
between suitcases on long rides
or on the backseat between Anne and Mel

when her father's hairy arm
swung back to stop a fight.
The same Sally who grew out

of her speech impediment by cutting out
pictures of cigarettes and scissors and repeating *S* words—
silly, sandy, sassafras with her speech teacher.

Sally who smoked cigarettes, found a home
in chemistry with Mr. Boehmler, got caught
in bed with a boy on the senior class trip,

becoming suspended-from-school Sally.
After all that, I went by my grandmother's name,
my given name, Sarah.

What I Would Do Were I in an Avalanche

Under a wave of snow
trapped in depth and bitter white,

I'd clear a space in front of my face to breathe
(of course) but also to drool. Whichever way

it runs on my cheek or chin, I'd dig in
the opposite direction—not Earth

but sky. Saliva signals, protects
as blood and muck

coat the newborn,
emerging from dark folds—

swaddled in waste and guts,
moving toward a light.

About the Author

Sarah Dickenson Snyder been writing poetry since she knew there was a form with conscious line breaks. Pertinent to her work as a writer, she has been an English teacher for many years, a mother for several, and a participant in poetry workshops. She was selected to be part of the Bread Loaf Writers' Conference. In May of 2016, she was a 30/30 Poet for Tupelo Press. Her chapbook, *Notes From a Nomad*, is forth coming by Finishing Line Press in 2017.